Made in United States
Orlando, FL
21 April 2022

17069105R00057